MW01673210

Original title:
Embrace Your Creativity

Editor: Jessica Elisabeth Luik
Author: Swan Charm
ISBN HARDBACK: 978-9916-86-302-2
ISBN PAPERBACK: 978-9916-86-303-9

Tides of Inspiration

Waves of thoughts in endless churn,
From depths unknown, ideas burn.
In silent whispers, dreams take flight,
Guided by the lunar light.

Upon the shores of mind's expanse,
Creation weaves its subtle dance.
Colors blend in vivid streams,
Painting life with boundless dreams.

Fires of Ingenuity

In the heart, a fervent flame,
Sparks of wonder, none the same.
Crafting worlds from ethereal air,
With vision's hand, we dare and dare.

Shapes and forms from minds ignite,
Forges blaze through darkest night.
In this heat, the world anew,
Born from fire, bright and true.

Map of Fantasies

Scrolls unrolled, horizons vast,
Mountains high and valleys cast.
Oceans deep with secrets bound,
On this map, a world profound.

Stars align in constellations bright,
Guiding travelers by their light.
Every symbol, tale untold,
In this realm, adventures bold.

A Realm Uncharted

Beyond the lines of known terrain,
Mysteries grow, wild and untamed.
Paths unwalked, we boldly tread,
In lands where dreams and shadows wed.

Echoes of the past entwine,
With futures that the brave define.
In twilight's glow, our spirits soar,
To realms uncharted, evermore.

Hidden Universes

In the depths where silence reigns,
Whispers form and worlds arise.
Stars are born in unseen lanes,
Mysteries conceal the skies.

Galaxies in shadows thrive,
Darkness holds the brightest lights.
Secrets in the void survive,
Infinite as endless nights.

In the realms where time is stilled,
Voices from the past resound.
Every shadow softly filled,
With the echoes, lost and found.

Textures of Thought

Waves of wisdom, tides of lore,
Thoughts like fabric gently woven.
Threads of insight, ever more,
Patterns form, a mind's unspoken.

Ideas shape the endless sea,
Ripples turn to currents deep.
Textures form, eternally,
Thoughts that wake or lull to sleep.

Within the canvas of the mind,
Brushstrokes paint a vivid hue.
Textures blending, intertwined,
Crafting worlds both old and new.

Dance of the Imagination

Twirl of dreams in twilight's grace,
Curtains rise to fantasy.
Dancers move in boundless space,
Steps align with mystery.

Wandering in realms unseen,
Paths of wonder, doors untold.
Imagination's endless scene,
Stories new and visions bold.

Wings of thoughts, they soar and glide,
Boundless skies of endless chase.
In this dance, the mind's own ride,
Every thought finds its own place.

Canvas of Dreams

Brush of starlight on the night,
Shades of wonder, hues of grace.
Canvas holds the dreams in sight,
Painting worlds in cosmic space.

Nighttime whispers, colors blend,
Vision forms where thoughts collide.
Infinite as dreams ascend,
Journey inwards, far and wide.

In the realm where dreams reside,
Every stroke a new creation.
Canvas fills from side to side,
Crafting life's own fascination.

Celestial Hand

In the velvet night, stars align,
Whispering secrets, ancient, divine.
A celestial hand envisions the sky,
Painting cosmos with a tranquil sigh.

Galaxies twirl in an astral dance,
Infinite wonders in every glance.
Through cosmic winds, stories unfold,
Æons of mysteries, silently told.

Nebulas shimmer with hues unseen,
Forging realms in a twilight sheen.
Comets blaze with a fiery brand,
Guided by the celestial hand.

Chromatic Dreams

In a world where colors blend and sway,
Chromatic dreams guide my way.
Hues of azure, shades of gold,
A vibrant tapestry to behold.

Rainbows stretch across the skies,
Mirroring hope in every guise.
Each shade a whisper, a promise new,
Infinite visions in every hue.

Painted whispers in twilight gleam,
Alive within this chromatic dream.
Vivid reflections of heart and mind,
In colors unspoken, beautifully entwined.

Sculpting Air

Invisible hands shape the air,
Breathing life into forms rare.
Through currents swift, their whispers glide,
Invisible art in motion, wide.

Zephyrs dance in silent grace,
Carving dreams in time and space.
Vapor trails and winds caress,
Crafting moments, pure finesse.

In the silent chorus, unseen,
Air becomes the sculptor's dream.
Shaping essence, light as air,
An ethereal touch, everywhere.

Phoenix in Ink

From ashes of prose, it rises true,
A phoenix in ink, reborn anew.
Feathers of verse, ignited bright,
Soaring through the endless night.

Words aflame with burning grace,
Traces of fire in every place.
Resurrecting tales, old and bold,
Stories of life, retold and enfold.

In every quill, a spark doth lie,
Awakening dreams, letting them fly.
From the embers of thought, on the brink,
Ascends the phoenix, crafted in ink.

Innovative Spirit

Within the mind, new worlds ignite,
Ideas dance in sheer delight.
Crafting futures, bold and bright,
Forging dreams in darkest night.

Curiosity's endless quest,
Rising high above the rest.
Innovation stands the test,
Passion's fire, ever blessed.

Imagination leads the way,
Guiding through both night and day.
Visions clear, with hues of gray,
Charting paths where hopes will stay.

Beneath the Quill

Ink flows gently, words take flight,
Weaving tales in darkest night.
Fiction dawns in pale moonlight,
Bringing worlds so sharp, so bright.

Pages whisper secrets old,
Stories written, tales retold.
Legends crafted, brave and bold,
Narratives in hands we hold.

Thoughts unspoken find their form,
In the heart, an endless storm.
Quill and paper, forever warm,
Lines of love, in prose transform.

Flights of Fancy

In the mind's eye, dragons soar,
Magic realms to be explored.
Castles rise, unseen before,
Mysteries behind each door.

Fairies dance on twilight beams,
Songs of wonder, woven seams.
Life resplendent in our dreams,
Fantasy in flowing streams.

Creatures wild in lush terrain,
Echoes of a sweet refrain.
Visions where the heart is lain,
Flights of fancy break the chain.

Elemental Vision

Wind's soft whisper through the trees,
Nature's music on the breeze.
Earth below, so firm it frees,
Rooted deep, our spirit sees.

Fire's burn ignites the soul,
Passion's ember, making whole.
Water's flow, its subtle toll,
Merges realms, complete control.

Elemental forces blend,
With the cosmos, minds transcend.
In their power, we defend,
Unity, on them depend.

The Muse's Call

In twilight's glow, the world unwinds,
A whisper stirs the soul confined.
The muse's call, a song divine,
Awakens dreams, where stars align.

Through shadowed woods and silver streams,
She beckons forth the deepest dreams.
A symphony of night and peace,
Where all life's wonders find release.

Her voice a balm, her spirit wild,
Guiding each wayward, searching child.
In silence, wisdom gently falls:
The heart responds to the muse's calls.

The Artist's Reverie

In quiet nooks of the artist's mind,
Where thoughts like rivers twist and wind,
Reality fades, a soft retreat,
Where past and future calmly meet.

Brushstrokes whisper tales untold,
Of skies afire and hues of gold.
Canvas cradles boundless skies,
Echoes of deep and ancient ties.

In reverie's embrace, truth reveals,
A world beyond what touch and feel.
With every stroke, the soul ignites,
In boundless realms of dream and light.

Tapestry of the Sublime

Woven threads of moments past,
In vibrant hues, a spell is cast.
Life's tapestry in colors fine,
Unfurls in patterns so divine.

Echoes of laughter, whispers of pain,
Entwined with sun, shadow, and rain.
Each memory, a thread so bright,
Glows softly in the fading light.

In the dance of time’s embrace,
We find ourselves in every place.
A rich design that both entwines,
And tells the tale of hearts and minds.

The Attic of Dreams

Up creaking stairs to attic's hold,
Where twilight turns the dust to gold.
Forgotten treasures, memory's gleams,
Lie dormant in the attic of dreams.

A chest of hopes, now long confined,
Awaits the seeker, heart inclined.
To open lids and let them free,
Unfolding tales of what could be.

Among the stars, beneath moon's beams,
Awakens now the attic's dreams.
A journey through the silent nights,
Where echoes turn to guiding lights.

Melody of Thoughts

In the garden where minds awake,
Notes of wisdom softly break.
Whispers dance in twilight's hue,
Melodies of thoughts ensue.

Streams of thought through valleys run,
As twilight fades, and day is won.
In the silence, truth is sought,
In the melody of thought.

Dreams take flight on fragile wings,
Imagination's chorus sings.
From the heart, the soul takes part,
Melody in every thought.

As night descends and shadows creep,
Mind’s orchestra gently sleeps.
In the stillness, notions sway,
Melodies that dawn the day.

Palette of Possibility

Colors blend in skies of dreams,
Infinite hues and whispered gleams.
Canvas of the future bright,
Palette of possibility's light.

Brushstrokes bold, horizons wide,
In colors deep, our hopes reside.
From every shade, a world anew,
Painted possibilities true.

In a drop of rain, a rainbow hides,
In every heart, potential tides.
With every hue, our spirits fly,
Toward the limitless, the sky.

Unfurling shades of day and night,
Possibilities in every light.
In every stroke, a moment free,
On life's grand canvas, we see.

Quill of Vision

In the silence of a winter's night,
Quill of vision starts its flight.
Across the vellum, dreams unfold,
Stories whispered, truths untold.

Ink flows free, a river wide,
Carving thoughts and dreams inside.
Vision blooms on parchment white,
Bringing shadows into light.

Imaginations take their form,
In the quiet, in the warm.
From the heart onto the page,
Quill releases, dreams engage.

Words take flight, like birds in spring,
On the quill, new visions sing.
In each line, a world is born,
Through the night, until the morn.

A Universe Woven

Stars align in cosmic threads,
Tales of old and futures spreads.
Patterns whispered, unseen sewn,
A universe of the unknown.

Across the night, threads intertwine,
Weaving worlds, a cosmic sign.
Galaxies in silence spin,
Mysteries in spacetime's skin.

In the fabric of the night,
Stars are pinpoints, tales of light.
Weaves the dark, a web profound,
In every star, new stories found.

Woven dreams in nebula's glow,
Cosmic beings ebb and flow.
In the vastness, threads are laid,
A universe of dreams portrayed.

Emerald Rhythms

In forests deep, where echoes play,
Emerald dreams come out to sway,
Leaves whisper tales of ancient lore,
Nature's song forevermore.

Sunlight filters through the green,
Glimmers dance in liquid sheen,
Footsteps light on mossy trails,
Winds serenade with gentle gales.

Brook and river softly sing,
Harmony in everything,
Emerald hues embrace the land,
Touched by nature's gentle hand.

Boughs that cradle birds in flight,
Dappled shades of morning light,
Peaceful whispers through the night,
Emerald rhythms pure and right.

As the day meets twilight's grace,
Nighttime cloaks the forest space,
In dreams of green we rest anew,
Emerald rhythms see us through.

Mind's Collage

In the gallery of the mind,
Memories and dreams combine,
Colors bright and shadows seem,
Part of an eternal scheme.

Pieces from a life once led,
Fragments of the words unsaid,
Images both bright and dim,
Form the art that lies within.

Thoughts that drift on winds of time,
Stories weave in silent rhyme,
Brushstrokes of a life bespoke,
Mind’s collage, a gentle cloak.

Moments fleeting, swift and light,
Captured in the pale moonlight,
Scenes that fade but never die,
Paintings in the inner eye.

Each reflection, every hue,
Marks of journeys old and new,
Mind’s collage, a sacred space,
Tracing life in gentle grace.

Ephemeral Art

In the fleeting breath of time,
Art emerges, so divine,
Ephemeral, it graces air,
Beauty flows without compare.

Moments captured, then they pass,
Like the breeze upon the grass,
Transient strokes of brilliance seen,
In a timeless, boundless dream.

Petals falling from a rose,
Snowflakes in their silent prose,
Fleeting scenes of beauty rare,
Ephemeral art laid bare.

Sunsets painting skies with fire,
Rainbows arch in soft attire,
Ephemeral art, a ghost,
Of a world that matters most.

Whispers of a passing thought,
Sculpted in a moment caught,
Art ephemeral, yet whole,
Imprints deep within the soul.

Infinity in Brushstrokes

Canvas wide and colors grand,
Brush in gentle, guiding hand,
Infinite the paths we see,
Through each painted mystery.

Each stroke tells a story's birth,
Endless skies and rolling earth,
In the lines, a universe,
Captured in a whispered verse.

Depths of oceans, stars that hum,
Mountains where the wild things run,
In the palette, worlds unfold,
Infinity in hues of gold.

Through each mark, a journey lies,
Hints of dreams and sweet goodbyes,
In the merging shades we see,
Brushstrokes paint eternity.

Art transcends the bounds of space,
In each stroke, a timeless grace,
Infinity in brushstrokes rare,
Beauty breathing, always there.

Gallery of Whimsy

In halls where dreams dance in disguise,
Colors swirl beneath twilight skies,
Whispers of laughter fill the air,
A world of wonder, beyond compare.

Each fresco spins a tale of light,
Pantomime of day and night,
Brushstrokes bold, and delicate beams,
Woven whims of fleeting dreams.

Through archways wide, the muses play,
In shadows cast by dawn's first ray,
A carnival of thoughts ascends,
Where imagination never ends.

Sculptures breathe with silent grace,
In every stone a hidden face,
Echoes of joy and soft embrace,
This gallery, a timeless space.

Step softly through this realm so rare,
Embark on flights of fancy fair,
In whims and fancies, be set free,
For here resides life's mystery.

Strokes of Genius

With hand and heart in fusion's fire,
A genesis of grand desire,
Canvas free, yet bounds portray,
The visions of the artist's way.

In hues that leap and winds that sigh,
A symphony beneath the sky,
The master's touch, a sacred brush,
Turns silence into fervent rush.

The soul laid bare in shades profound,
Each line, a whisper, shape, a sound,
In genius found, and spirit's flight,
The dark turned bright by inner light.

From void to life, each stroke reveals,
The beating heart that never kneels,
In triumphs small and battles grand,
We see the world within one's hand.

In every masterpiece, a glance,
At timeless truths and thought's expanse,
Thus etched upon the scrolls of time,
A genius' touch, forever sublime.

Infinite Possibilities

Beneath the arch of endless skies,
Where dreams take wing and visions rise,
Horizons new in dawn's embrace,
A symphony of boundless space.

Each thought a spark, potential pure,
In realms unseen lies all allure,
The threads of fate, so finely spun,
Compose the dance of earth and sun.

In atoms small and stars so bright,
Existence pulses, day and night,
The pathways forged by minds unchained,
Unfold in wonders unexplained.

Here, every choice, a forked path winds,
A tapestry that fate designs,
We weave with will and daring heart,
The endless realms where we take part.

Embrace the infinite unknown,
Where seeds of thought have always grown,
For all we yearn and hope to be,
Exists within possibility.

Echoes of Vision

In twilight's soft, embracing hue,
Visions spark, wondrously new,
Echoes of thought in silent waves,
Dancing in dreamlike enclaves.

Through mist and shadow, light reveals,
The heart's true call, the soul's appeals,
Mirrored fields that gleam and glow,
In vision's realm, wise whispers flow.

In every glance, a world perceived,
Where shadows fade and hopes conceived,
The echoes rise of distant shores,
Unlocking all unseen doors.

With inner sight, the path divine,
Is traced in lines of light and time,
The whispers guide, the echoes sing,
Of visions vast and endless spring.

Embrace the depth within the gaze,
Where echoes of the vision blaze,
For in those depths, the future's cast,
A boundless view, forever vast.

Hidden Cadences

In the still of silent nights,
Whispers carry ancient lore,
Echoes of forgotten fights,
Songs sung by the ocean's roar.

Beneath the surface, rhythms hide,
Unseen pulses of the day,
Life’s compositions, amplified,
In every breath that winds its way.

Mysteries wrapped in lullabies,
Verses spun with secret threads,
Each note a truth that underlies,
The music where the spirit treads.

Cadences unsaid, unseen,
Compose a world of hidden sound,
Where every moment has serene,
A harmony that's so profound.

Let your heart’s own pendulum,
Swing to beats of timeless grace,
For in this silent, secret hum,
Hidden cadences find their place.

Frame of Epiphanies

Moments caught in crystal light,
Glimmers of an inner shine,
Revelations soft and bright,
Within the mind's expanding line.

A blink, a thought, a sudden glance,
Unlocks a door to hidden realms,
In every fleeting happenstance,
A sailor steers and takes the helm.

Frames of time where wisdom dwells,
Snapshots of eternity,
From the silence where it wells,
Springs a new serenity.

Shifting shades of whispered dreams,
Paint a canvas vast and wide,
Where nothing is quite as it seems,
Yet each is truth defined inside.

In these frames, epiphanies,
Glide like seagulls on the breeze,
Witness miracles arise,
And find the wonder in the ease.

Sculptors of the Ether

Hands that mold the unseen air,
Crafting visions out of naught,
Shaping dreams with gentle care,
In the realm where thoughts are caught.

Artists weave the void with grace,
Touching whispers woven fine,
Creating worlds in cosmic space,
With strokes of light, their grand design.

Chiseling the nothingness,
Bringing form to shapeless mist,
Conjuring with mindfulness,
A universe that can't resist.

Freedoms forged in boundless flight,
In domains of purest thought,
Masters of the infinite night,
Sculpting truths that can't be bought.

In this ether, endless skies,
Crafted by such deft decree,
Sculptors render mystic ties,
Binding souls eternally.

Infinite Pathways

Wander down the endless road,
Forking trails of possibility,
Every step, a new abode,
Echoes of infinity.

In the maze of divergent ways,
Choices bloom like morning flowers,
Every twist another phase,
A dance within life’s golden hours.

Beneath the stars, the paths expand,
Boundless routes of destiny,
Lines in the desert, traced in sand,
Maps of cosmic symphony.

Journey on through veils of night,
And wander with an open heart,
For in the dark, there shines delight,
A lantern's glow to play its part.

Infinite pathways, they unwind,
In every step, the cosmos sings,
Follow them, and you will find,
Eternity on fleeting wings.

Visionaries' Realm

In dreams where seekers dare to tread,
A realm of wonders lies ahead.
Through mist and time, with vision's gleam,
They walk the pathways of a dream.

Stars above, like mindful guides,
Paint the skies with light that bides.
Upon this land of hopes untold,
The future's secrets they behold.

Mountains whisper ancient lore,
Oceans sing of distant shores.
In their hearts, the dreamers see,
A world that yet shall rise to be.

With every step, a spark ignites,
A constellation in the nights.
Boundless are the skies they sail,
In the visionaries' hallowed tale.

Secrets of the Unseen

Beneath the veil of mundane sight,
Lies a realm as dark as night.
Hidden truths, the world has known,
In shadows where the whispers groan.

Ancient trees with wise old eyes,
Hold the secrets of the skies.
In their leaves, the wind conspires,
To fan the flames of hidden fires.

In the stillness, voices blend,
Stories merge, and rivers bend.
Every grain of sand reveals,
Mysteries that time conceals.

Nighttime sets the stage for dreams,
Where nothing's ever as it seems.
Unlock the cryptic, golden key,
And glimpse the unseen's majesty.

Enchanted Musings

In the quiet of twilight's glow,
Where shadows dance and soft winds blow,
A whispered thought, a fleeting sigh,
Takes wing beneath the azure sky.

Magic whirls in the moonlit haze,
Casting light on secret ways.
Dreams begin their silent flight,
In the musings of the night.

Ancient chants the stars recite,
Weaving spells of endless light.
Nature hums a lullaby,
Of mysteries that fade and fly.

Come, wander through the starlit mist,
Feel the night with a gentle twist.
Listen close, the musings say,
In this world, there's magic at play.

Fields of Possibility

Endless fields of golden grain,
Stretch across the vast terrain.
Every breeze, a whispered chance,
Of fate's impulsive, hidden dance.

Dreamers stroll these fertile lands,
Hopeful hearts and open hands.
In the soil, they plant their dreams,
Nurtured by the sunlight's beams.

Skies above, a canvas wide,
Where visions soar and futures ride.
Every star, a beacon bright,
Guides the way through endless night.

Paths untraveled, roads untaken,
Possibilities awaken.
With faith and toil, we'll see them grow,
In fields where endless hopes will sow.

Chasing Rainbows

Beneath the clouds so grey and vast,
A spectrum bright, a moment cast,
We chase the hues that fade too fast,
In hopes that they forever last.

Through meadows lush and valleys deep,
We wander where the colors sleep,
In twilight's grasp where shadows creep,
And secrets in the raindrops seep.

Horizons wide and dreams anew,
With every turn a different view,
The sky unveils its vibrant rue,
A palette of the morning dew.

In whispers soft, the breezes tell,
Of prisms born where lovers dwell,
We follow where the rainbows fell,
Enchantments break the twilight’s spell.

Endless skies, our hearts in tow,
We tread the paths that few may know,
In search of where the rainbows grow,
We find the light within their glow.

Threads of Silver

On tapestries of night unfold,
Where stars of silver stories told,
Threads of dreams in webs they hold,
A timeless dance in skies so bold.

Whispered hues of twilight fade,
In moonlit realms where shadows played,
Through silken strands in light arrayed,
Echoes of the nights portrayed.

Beneath the weaver's careful hand,
The stars align in cosmic band,
A silver thread through timeless sands,
We trace the patterns life has planned.

Soft serenades on breezes flow,
Their ancient songs of long ago,
In silver threads the secrets show,
Of life’s rich tapestries we know.

In twilight’s loom our dreams they weave,
A dance of light we all perceive,
Through silver threads our hearts believe,
In constellations we conceive.

Spirit of Creation

In moments still, ideas ignite,
A spark within the endless night,
The spirit wakes to strike the light,
And shadows take their flight in sight.

Brush in hand, the artist stands,
With every stroke the world expands,
In colors bright from distant lands,
The canvas breathes as heart commands.

A sculptor’s touch, in stone or clay,
From silent forms, life finds its way,
In chiseled lines the voices say,
Creation sings in night and day.

Word by word the poet's dream,
Weaves through minds in silent stream,
In every line, a new extreme,
A universe where thoughts redeem.

The spirit of creation flows,
In every heart where passion sows,
Through endless time the essence grows,
In acts of love the spirit shows.

Ink and Soul

Ink and soul entwined together,
Through stormy nights and tranquil weather,
The pen it touches truth like feather,
In words that bind us close forever.

Pages filled with thoughts unspoken,
Heartfelt vows that can't be broken,
In quiet moments, softly awoken,
A testament to love's unbroken.

In every book a journey lies,
Written stars in endless skies,
Through every tear and every rise,
The ink reveals where truth belies.

With every stroke the essence beams,
Of lives lived and all their dreams,
In prose and verse, in silent streams,
The ink and soul fulfill their schemes.

Through ink and soul we find a way,
To speak the words we long to say,
In boundless realms where dreams convey,
Our hearts in written lines portray.

Blueprints of Wonder

In the silence, whispers call,
Designs in twilight's gentle thrall.
Dreams trace paths, unseen, untold,
In realms where hearts and stars unfold.

Mercury-hued scribes of night,
Penning fables in the twilight.
Mystic codes in azure scrolls,
Woven through with silver soul.

Shapes emerge in shadows' weave,
Wonders others won't believe.
Blueprints sketched by moonlight cast,
Stories of a time long past.

Through the veil of midnight's song,
Timeless echoes drift along.
Wonders dance in cosmic glow,
In secret patterns few shall know.

Voyages in dreams take flight,
Where ink and stardust reunite.
Blueprints forged in night’s embrace,
Etching beauty, finding grace.

Echoes of Inner Worlds

Within the quiet mind's expanse,
Echoes weave a silent dance.
Voices from our hidden core,
Speak in whispers, forever more.

Mirrored realms reflect inside,
Echoes of where truths reside.
In the calm, a vast domain,
Boundless thoughts like endless rain.

Shadows play where light refrains,
Scarred yet pure, the heart remains.
A labyrinth of dreams and fears,
Building bridges through the years.

Echoes of our deepest cries,
Born in silence, where we lie.
Timeless wisdom, softly spun,
Carried 'til the day is done.

In the echo, secrets find,
Paths that intertwine the mind.
Journeys through the soul's domain,
Echoes lingering, like refrain.

Alchemy of Thought

Fragments of a silver muse,
Blend in alchemy's amuse.
Thoughts transforming lead to gold,
In secrets, ancient truths unfold.

Mind's philosopher's refrain,
Chasing wisdom, capturing pain.
Turning doubts to sterling rays,
In this dance of mental praise.

Through the crucible of time,
Alchemy of thought shall climb.
Melding hope, dissolving fears,
Crafting worlds through silent tears.

Transmutations of the soul,
In the void, we find our role.
Shapeless dreams take solid form,
In the heart where thoughts are born.

Alchemy of thought’s embrace,
Threads of mind in cosmic space.
Universe in every spark,
Mirrored in our deepest dark.

Symphony of Invention

Notes that rise on twilight breeze,
Weaving through the forest trees.
Invention's symphony awaits,
Opening wide creation's gates.

Gears and dreams both intertwine,
In the heart's inventive mind.
Crafting melodies so rare,
Wonders born from tender care.

Harmony of thought and light,
Dancing in invention's flight.
Symphonies unseen, yet known,
In every mind, a seed is sown.

In the rhythm, shadows play,
Carving out a brighter day.
Invention's voice, a nuanced call,
Eternal vastness, in it all.

Symphony of pure design,
Crafted in the clearest mind.
Notes of wonder, born anew,
Symphony's endless rendezvous.

Whispers of the Imagination

In twilight's embrace, where shadows play,
Dreams drift softly like clouds of gray.
Whispers of worlds in silent streams,
Awaken realms of endless dreams.

Stars twinkle tales of yesteryears,
In the hush of night, no space for fears.
Echoes of laughter, whispers of cries,
Blend in the canvas of starlit skies.

Thoughts take flight on wings unseen,
Exploring the realms of might-have-been.
In the tapestry of the mind's embrace,
Each whisper finds its secret place.

Rivers of wonder, lakes of lore,
In the silence, imaginations soar.
Beyond the veil where reality sleeps,
Lie the secrets the imagination keeps.

Voices of old whisper through time,
Crafting verses in rhythm and rhyme.
Where silence speaks in tones so deep,
Imagination's secrets softly creep.

Canvas of Dreams

Upon the canvas, wide and bare,
Dreams are woven with tender care.
Brushes whisper secrets untold,
In colors warm and hues so bold.

Morning light with gentle gleam,
Infuses life into every dream.
Each stroke a wish, a silent prayer,
Reflecting hopes, dispelling despair.

Mountains high and valleys low,
In dreams, the boundaries cease to grow.
Oceans vast and skies of blue,
The canvas holds a world anew.

Stories painted with silent grace,
Evoke the past, the heart's embrace.
Visions crafted in twilight's beams,
Reside in the canvas of our dreams.

Threads of light and shadows gray,
Confess the night's and dawn's ballet.
In this realm where limits cease,
Dreams find a moment of peaceful release.

Wings of Innovation

From fires of thought and sparks of mind,
Ideas blossom, breaking old confines.
Wings of innovation rise in flight,
Chasing dawn in the heart of night.

Secrets of science, lore of art,
Merge and mend where dreams depart.
Inventions born from questions deep,
Break the silence where answers sleep.

Boundaries fall like evening rain,
Creativity flows from core to brain.
From ancient roots to future's quest,
On wings of change we are truly blessed.

Through trial and error, risks are sown,
Foundations of progress remain unknown.
Yet in each failure, wisdom hides,
Guiding innovations' endless tides.

In halls of thought and fields of green,
Imagination reigns supreme.
The wings of progress never cease,
Charting paths where dreams and truths unleash.

Brushstrokes of the Soul

Colors dance on the palette's brim,
Each stroke begins a quiet hymn.
The artist's heart, with passion whole,
Reveals the brushstrokes of the soul.

Emerald greens and azure blues,
Capture life's many hues.
In every line, a story told,
A glimpse of secrets, silent and bold.

Moments of joy, whispers of pain,
Find solace on the canvas' plane.
Each emotion, raw and true,
Is painted in a unique hue.

From dawn's blush to twilight's hue,
The soul's brush reveals a view.
Life's essence in colors profound,
Is gently laid on sacred ground.

With every stroke, a tale unfolds,
Of life, and love, and secrets untold.
In art's embrace, the soul finds peace,
In colors, the heart's whispers cease.

Gardens of Creation

In the heart of fertile lands, life awakens,
Petals bloom as the dawn-tide quakes,
Roots descend, in the earth they are taken,
Whispering tales of what life forsakes.

Waters gleam under the kiss of the moon,
Leaves rustle in harmonic suspense,
Nature's orchestra, playing a tune,
Gardens of creation, blooming immense.

Insects hum, a song of persistence,
Colors dance in air, vibrant and light,
Whispers of wind tell of existence,
Gardens of creation, merging day and night.

Sunlight filters through the canopy tall,
Seeds hold dreams of tomorrows new,
Grass blades tremble, answering the call,
To grow, to flourish, under skies blue.

Paths entwine, stones of wisdom laid,
In these gardens, all seasons meet,
A cycle of life, never to fade,
Creation's masterpiece, endlessly sweet.

Luminescent Whimsy

Glittering softly, stars adorn the skies,
Whispers of night in celestial prose,
Moonbeam dances, light in disguise,
Casting dreams where the sea breeze blows.

Fairies shimmer in the twilight's gleam,
Chasing shadows of the woodland sprite,
In a world built on whimsical dream,
Drifting softly through the velvet night.

Oceans reflect a silvery trail,
Luminescent paths guiding the way,
Through waves that sing a siren's wail,
In a dance with the twilight's array.

In the heart of a midnight garden,
Where the lily's glow is soft and bright,
Magic weaves its endless pardon,
In threads of luminescent light.

Mystery hums in the quiet gloom,
Stars converse with the earthly kin,
In the heart of night's gentle bloom,
Lives the whimsy hidden within.

Treasures in the Mind

Hidden deep within the folds of thought,
Lies treasures time cannot erode,
Memories of battles bravely fought,
In the depths, where true riches bode.

Dreams unfurling like a gossamer thread,
Ideas sprouting, ever so kind,
In the shadows of what has been said,
Lie treasures yet to be mined.

Wisdom bound in tomes of old,
Words whispered in tones so wise,
Stories of courage, hearts bold,
In the annals of the mind's vast skies.

Creativity dances on cerebral waves,
Imagination knows no strict confines,
In every thought, a secret it saves,
Mapping treasures in mental mines.

Through synapses, electric flows,
Connections form, a spark of the divine,
In the garden where intellect grows,
Lie the treasures of the mind's design.

Fusion of Imagery

Brushstrokes blend hues on canvas bright,
Sunset's glow with the ocean's tide,
Moments captured in the waning light,
In colors, memories reside.

Words like paint, on a page they spread,
Crafting visions in each reader's mind,
Fusion of imagery, where thoughts are led,
In the harmony of art combined.

Every scene a verse, every rhyme a shade,
Poetry and painting, intertwined,
From the strokes, a symphony is made,
In the souls of those aligned.

Nature's palette, reflecting life's call,
Mountains, rivers in sentences sown,
Fusion of imagery, uniting them all,
In a masterpiece, effortlessly grown.

Worlds converge in the artist's heart,
Where dreams and reality entwine,
In the fusion where all forms take part,
Creating beauty, pure and divine.

Muse Beyond Measure

In twilight's gentle, softened hue,
Where stars begin their nightly waltz,
A muse of infinite expanse,
Breathes life into the world at dusk.

In whispered winds, her voice takes flight,
Revealing tales of land and sea,
A canvas stretched across the night,
Paints dreams of boundless mystery.

With every brush, and every hue,
She weaves the magic, thread by thread,
A tapestry of night’s allure,
Where endless thoughts and visions spread.

The heart of night, her spirit glows,
A beacon in the quiet dark,
Guiding souls through unseen paths,
Imprinting love, like embers’ spark.

So when the night envelopes all,
And silence holds the world in thrall,
Remember muse’s soft caress,
Her whisper, life’s enthralling call.

Glowing Embers

Within the hearth, a quiet glow,
Where stories dance in amber's flame,
A warmth that whispers old and new,
And sparks that whisper every name.

In glowing embers, tales arise,
Of ancient lands and distant skies,
A touch of past, a hint of now,
In every flicker lies the wise.

The hearth, a keeper of the lore,
A sentinel of time and more,
Each ember holds a secret’s key,
Unlocking worlds we’ve yet to see.

Echoes of laughter, sighs of pain,
All flicker in the flame’s domain,
A mirror to the heart’s own fire,
Reflecting love, life’s true desire.

So let the embers softly glow,
In quiet peace and fervent show,
A constant in the flow of time,
A whisper in life’s gentle rhyme.

Reverie in Design

In quiet moments, thoughts align,
Imaginations intertwine,
A reverie, a grand design,
Of visions dancing, pure and fine.

The architect of dreams takes flight,
With canvases of day and night,
With every brushstroke, every line,
A new world forms in soft delight.

Each design, a story told,
In patterns subtle, bright and bold,
A delicate, intricate thread,
Weaving dreams inside the head.

Through curves and lines, the mind explores,
A universe without closed doors,
Creating endless possibilities,
In worlds of boundless novelties.

So in the quiet, let thoughts weave,
A tapestry beyond belief,
A reverie where minds find peace,
In designs where wonders never cease.

Journeys of the Heart

Through fields of gold and skies so blue,
The heart embarks on journeys new,
In every beat, a step so true,
A path that's endless, ever due.

The road may wind, the hills may climb,
In rhythm with the heart's own time,
With each new dawn, a fresh pursuit,
In search of life's most cherished truth.

In valleys deep and mountains high,
The heart finds strength, learns how to fly,
Through trials and joy, the journey's course,
Is guided by an unseen force.

With every beat, a story grown,
A legacy of love is sown,
The heart's own journey, pure and vast,
A faithful echo of the past.

So let the heart's adventures start,
Embrace the world, its lessons chart,
For in the journey, life's true art,
Is found within the beating heart.

Arcane Symphony

Beneath the twilight's gentle gaze,
Sings the symphony of old days,
Where shadows dance in mystic haze,
And secrets whisper through the maze.

Celestial notes in midnight's breath,
Compose the song that conquers death,
With every star, a chord is spun,
In harmonic chains the worlds are won.

Through forests deep and oceans wide,
The arcs of time and fate collide,
In melodies unseen, unheard,
By mortal eyes or earthly word.

Chasing dreams on wings of gold,
The tales of yore they do unfold,
In cryptic chords and ancient prose,
The arcane symphony forever flows.

Spirit of Fantasy

In lands where magic weaves the air,
A spirit dances, wild and fair,
With wings of light and dreams so rare,
In realms of fantasy, unaware.

Mountains whisper ancient lore,
As rivers sing to distant shores,
In every breeze, the legends soar,
Of dragons, knights, and battles' roar.

The stars alight on night's embrace,
Ignite the tales of time and space,
In every heart, a sacred place,
For words of wonder and of grace.

With every dawn, a story new,
In every dusk, the colors true,
Inflame the skies in varied hue,
The spirit of fantasy breaks through.

Multi-Hued Whispers

In gardens where the flowers bloom,
A symphony of colors loom,
Their whispers dance through nature's room,
A canvas painted by the loom.

Each petal tells a tale untold,
In palettes rich, in hues so bold,
Emerald greens and purples old,
And crimson hearts of stories sold.

Within the silent breath of morn,
The dewdrops' prism, sunlight born,
Reveal the whispers, softly worn,
On rainbows' arch, the dreams are sworn.

Through changing leaves and sky's disguise,
The whispers float, the shades arise,
In every gaze and every sigh,
Multi-hued whispers mesmerize.

Creative Metamorphosis

In the cocoon of thoughts and dreams,
Where nothing's ever as it seems,
Ideas sprout like gentle streams,
In whispering winds and moonlit gleams.

Through strokes of brush and pen's embrace,
The mind transforms, it sets the pace,
In colors bold and forms that trace,
A universe in every space.

Metamorphosis takes its flight,
In shadowed day, in radiant night,
With every change, a new insight,
To realms unknown and endless light.

Imagination soars and spins,
In boundless spheres where art begins,
Forever turning, shedding skins,
Creative power never thins.

Moments Reimagined

In the silence, whispers lie,
Moments fleeting, shadows fly.
Dreams awaken, hearts anew,
In the stillness, visions grew.

Colors blend in twilight's glaze,
Timeless echoes, endless maze.
Across dimensions, time will mend,
Moments past and those we send.

Glimmers lost in morning's glaze,
Collecting stardust from sun's rays.
Infinite, the morning sighs,
Weaving tapestries in skies.

Secrets woven in the night,
Moonlit paths in silver light.
Glancing back, the past rephrased,
Moments danced and reappraised.

From a seedling's tender might,
Moments sprout within our sight.
Threads of life, reimagined blend,
In every moment, worlds extend.

Evolving Wonder

Behold the dawn, the world reborn,
Each petal soft, the edge adorned.
Life emerges, colors sprung,
In the heart where echoes sung.

Mysteries in nature's scroll,
Wisdom wrapped in gentle fold.
Evolving paths, the journey wide,
In wonder's eyes, the truths reside.

Waves of time in ebb and flow,
In each gust, fresh whispers blow.
Around the bends, in winds so free,
Evolving wonder waits to see.

Sacred cycles, turning wheels,
In the spiral, the essence heals.
Chrysalis in dreams unfurl,
Evolving truth in hidden pearl.

Nested close, the stars align,
Evolving stories intertwined.
In the realm where wonders thrive,
Endless marvels come alive.

Inspiration's Harvest

Fields of gold in morning haze,
Seeds of hope the sun will praise.
Inspiration grows in light,
Leaves of thought take soaring flight.

Plow the depths of hearts unseen,
Harvest dreams where love has been.
Fertile ground of souls entwined,
Inspiration's warmth, refined.

In the fields of endless grace,
Every dawn a sweet embrace.
Harvest whispers through the air,
Inspiration's bounty rare.

Beneath the sky, creations rise,
Ideas bloom in open skies.
In each furrow, sparks ignite,
Inspiration's glowing light.

Gathered close in twilight's calm,
Inspiration's soothing balm.
A harvest rich, a spirit's yield,
Inspiration's truths revealed.

Crystals of Fantasy

In realms of dreams, the rivers flow,
Where fabled luminescence glow.
Crystals dance on moonlit beams,
Twinkling lights in fantasy's dreams.

Whispers of the ancient trees,
Soft as summer’s gentle breeze.
Fables woven in the air,
Crystals sparkle, pure and rare.

Journey far in twilight's realm,
Magic guides and stars at helm.
Fantasy in crystal streams,
Worlds anew in mystic dreams.

Through the veils of time they wind,
Crystals glisten, tales in kind.
Sparkling paths that lead the way,
Fantasy’s pure light of day.

From the shadows, light will beam,
In the crystals, our dreams gleam.
Threads of myth in life's grand sea,
Crystals of our fantasy.

Sparks of Genius

A fleeting thought, a sudden flame,
Illuminates the darkened frame.
From deep abyss, a light ascends,
An idea glows, the mind transcends.

With every spark, a realm unfolds,
A world uncharted, tales untold.
In moments brief, the visions soar,
Creation's seed in mind's vast lore.

Ephemeral yet so profound,
The silent whisper, without sound.
From void to form, the shapes align,
Crafting wonders, so divine.

In twilight hues, brilliance gleams,
Guiding souls through endless dreams.
An ember's touch, ignites a blaze,
Through mystic realms, the spirit sways

Awake the muse, let thoughts conspire,
Fueling the heart, with pure desire.
In every spark, a genius lies,
Transforming whispers into skies.

Mosaic of the Mind

Fragments of a shattered whole,
Pieces of the heart and soul.
Colorful, the shards align,
Crafting tales, through space and time.

Each piece a story, carved in light,
Memories sewn, in patterns bright.
Together, form a tapestry,
Of dreams and thoughts, in harmony.

In every crack, a lesson gleaned,
Wisdom found through seams unseen.
The mind a canvas, vast and wide,
Where myriad hues of life reside.

Embrace the chaos, find the form,
A fragile beauty, in the norm.
The perfect blend of order, wild,
Within the psyche, tamed yet riled.

In splinters, lies the grand design,
A mosaic of the realm divine.
Unified, the fragments bind,
The limitless expanse of the mind.

Verses of Vision

In ink and quill, the dreams unfold,
A canvas vast, in words retold.
The verses sing, of realms unseen,
Of hidden worlds, and magic's sheen.

Each line a whisper, from the stars,
Guiding through the cosmic scars.
In every rhyme, a portal's grace,
A journey to another place.

Through twilight halls of thought we glide,
Where truth and illusion coincide.
The pen, a scepter, ruling realms,
With every stroke, the mind overwhelms.

Immortal thoughts on pages lie,
Transcending time, they never die.
In verses deep, our visions soar,
Unlocking dreams forevermore.

The poet's heart, a boundless sea,
Crafting worlds yet meant to be.
In every word, the visions rise,
A kaleidoscope beneath the skies.

Labyrinth of Ideas

In winding paths, thoughts intertwine,
A maze within, where shadows shine.
Through corridors of hopes and fears,
Whispers echo, through the years.

With every turn, a question springs,
A riddle, bound with silent strings.
The mind explores, seeks to unwind,
The tangled web of the designed.

In darkness, light begins to gleam,
Ideas dance, like a waking dream.
Each corner holds a mystery,
Each pathway to a history.

From chaos, patterns start to form,
A logic found within the storm.
In every twist, a new insight,
Guiding through the endless night.

The labyrinth, though vast and deep,
Holds secrets for the bold to reap.
In every thought, a spark, a flame,
Within the maze, ideas reclaim.

Fantasy's Brush

In twilight's gentle, amber hue,
A world of dreams begins anew,
Where whispers dance on evening's breath,
And stars sketch stories with deft.

The moonlight paints with silver sheen,
A land unseen, where thoughts convene,
Through forests deep and oceans wide,
Adventures born on fantasy's tide.

A dragon's flame, a lover's sigh,
In this realm, where spirits fly,
Mysteries fold in clouds above,
Crafted by hand, with endless love.

Wings unfurl on wind's soft kiss,
Mystic lands in twilight's bliss,
Brushed with stardust, realms unfold,
Tales of wonder yet untold.

Epiphanies in Color

Splash of azure, hint of green,
Nature's palette, ever keen,
With each stroke, a story told,
In colors rich, and pure, and bold.

Amber hues at dawn's first light,
Whispers of the coming night,
Brushes bleed in crimson hues,
As day departs, a deeper muse.

Canvas bright with thoughts unleashed,
Epiphanies in colors pieced,
Each shade reveals a hidden truth,
A blend of life, and art, and youth.

Swirling skies and rivers bend,
Ephemeral, yet without end,
In the heart of every scene,
Lies epiphany, serene.

Architect of Ideas

Foundations built in thoughts profound,
Ideas take flight, unbound,
With blueprints drawn in endless dreams,
A world is shaped by wisdom's beams.

Through mind's vast hallways echoes sound,
In quiet, brilliance often found,
Each structure born from concepts bright,
Emerging pure, in endless light.

Arches high and towers beam,
Each crafted from a fleeting dream,
As visions mold the air and stone,
An architect's heart is clearly shown.

Blueprints of imagination,
Spark profound creation,
In the chambers of the mind,
A world anew, designed.

Beneath the Surface

Beneath thc mirror's quiet sheen,
Lies a world of untold scene,
In depths unseen by fleeting eyes,
A universe of hidden skies.

Ripples trace a tale untold,
Of mysteries in waters cold,
Where life unfolds in shadows deep,
And secrets silently do keep.

In liquid halls, a dance of grace,
Creatures glide with phantom's face,
Veins of rivers, oceans wide,
Hold the truths the waves confide.

Deep within, the silence hums,
A hidden song in tenor's drums,
Beneath the surface, myriad lies,
A treasure trove 'neath tranquil skies.

Flights in Frame

In skies where dreams entwine,
With wings of painted hue,
The heavens grant us passage,
To realms where hearts renew.

Across the azure canvas,
We trace the paths of light,
Where sun and stars together,
Illuminate the night.

Horizons seem to whisper,
Of lands and times unknown,
Each cloud a fleeting moment,
In journeys we've outgrown.

In frames of fleeting glimpses,
We capture flights of fate,
The world beneath us slumbers,
As we transcend the weight.

The wind becomes our story,
The sky our boundless page,
In every whispered current,
Our spirits disengage.

Shadows of Thought

In recesses of the mind,
Where whispers softly tread,
Shadows weave their quiet tales,
In places seldom read.

The echoes of reflections,
In corridors of time,
Unveil the depths of wonder,
With thoughts that dare to climb.

They dance in silent stillness,
Where light and dark embrace,
A symphony of silence,
In thought's profoundest grace.

With shadows ever shifting,
We find our truths revealed,
In layers of the unseen,
Our innermost concealed.

The subtle hues of thinking,
In shadows softly fall,
They tell the untold stories,
Within the mind's high wall.

Aspirations in Abstract

Beyond the painted surface,
Where colors intertwine,
Lie dreams in vibrant motion,
Through abstract, they define.

Each stroke a whispered promise,
Each hue a silent vow,
In canvases of longing,
Our hopes take shape somehow.

The realms of pure creation,
Where visions freely roam,
Invite the soul to wander,
And find a fleeting home.

The chaos finds its order,
In aspirations grand,
With every abstract contour,
The dreams extend a hand.

A tapestry of wonder,
In vibrant, swirling hues,
We find our aspirations,
In abstract's candid muse.

Transcending Boundaries

We walk the edge of wonders,
Where limits are unknown,
The boundaries once constraining,
To fragments are now blown.

In fields of endless vision,
Our spirits take to flight,
We cross the lines of distance,
Into the boundless night.

With every daring venture,
We test the unknown space,
And find in each new crossing,
A glimpse of boundless grace.

The chains that once confine us,
Dissolve in earnest quest,
As boundaries become whispers,
In hearts that seek no rest.

We rise beyond the finite,
On paths both wild and free,
Transcending every boundary,
As far as dreams can see.

Inventing Tomorrow

Whispers of stardust guide the way,
Dreams merge with the dawn's first light.
Innovation cast in gentle clay,
Future's blueprint, bold and bright.

A symphony of minds, create,
Uncharted realms, they dare to thread.
Each idea, a sparkling fate,
Invention's call, by passion led.

Through valleys deep and mountains high,
The quest for new horizons raced.
With every spark, we touch the sky,
Unknown paths, with courage faced.

Tomorrow's canvas, pure and wide,
Brushstrokes of hope and daring gleam.
Together, onward we will stride,
Inventors bound by shared dream.

Our journey’s tale yet to unfold,
In the deep echoes of the morrow.
Wonders await, as we are bold,
In minds, a world we borrow.

Stories in Motion

Pages turn, a life unfurls,
Each word a heartbeat, clear and strong.
In tales of love, in distant worlds,
Our souls find where they belong.

Characters, in shadows bright,
Dance to melodies of lore.
In every chapter, day and night,
New wonders wait to explore.

The ink, like rivers, flows and weaves,
Binding tales both old and new.
Each storyteller, who believes,
Brings their visions forth in view.

A caravan of dreams that glide,
Through pages worn, and pages crisp.
In ink, our deepest hopes reside,
Across each written, whispered lisp.

Forevermore, the stories chase,
In hearts, a never-ending flight.
In prose or verse, they leave a trace,
Lit by the softest evening light.

Spectrum of Thought

Colors blend in mind's embrace,
Ideas weave a vivid seam.
In rainbow arcs of endless trace,
Ephemeral, like morning's dream.

From dusk till dawn, the thoughts arise,
Resplendent hues, in silent stream.
Each notion, art beneath closed eyes,
A spectrum wide, in constant gleam.

Imagination’s vast expanse,
A palette rich, no bounds confined.
In every thought, a chance to dance,
To revel in what’s undefined.

Spectrum of thought, a boundless sea,
Where colors shift with ev'ry tide.
From twilight to infinity,
In mental hues, we seek and hide.

With minds alight, we paint the night,
In visions clear, or shadowed nought.
A canvas bright of purest sight,
Eternal spectrum, ever sought.

Colors Unconfined

In the cradle of dawn, colors bloom,
Unfurling wings, beyond the sky.
No boundaries within their room,
In endless flight, they rise and fly.

Vibrant strokes, on life’s grand stage,
Painter’s palette, nature’s hand.
Ever-shifting, breaking cage,
In wild embrace, our hearts expand.

The hues of joy, the shades of woe,
Each emotion, brightly cast.
Together they electrify, bestow,
A masterpiece, in moments vast.

Unconfined by lines or frames,
They spread their whispers, touch the soul.
All colors cherishing their names,
In unity, they make us whole.

So let the colors free to roam,
In open skies, their true design.
For in their dance, we find our home,
A world of shades, profoundly divine.

Printed in the USA
CPSIA information can be obtained
at www.ICGtesting.com
LVHW020311040824
787202LV00001B/259

9 789916 863039